Find the hidden pictures.

AF089582

b a c e

yellow green brown red

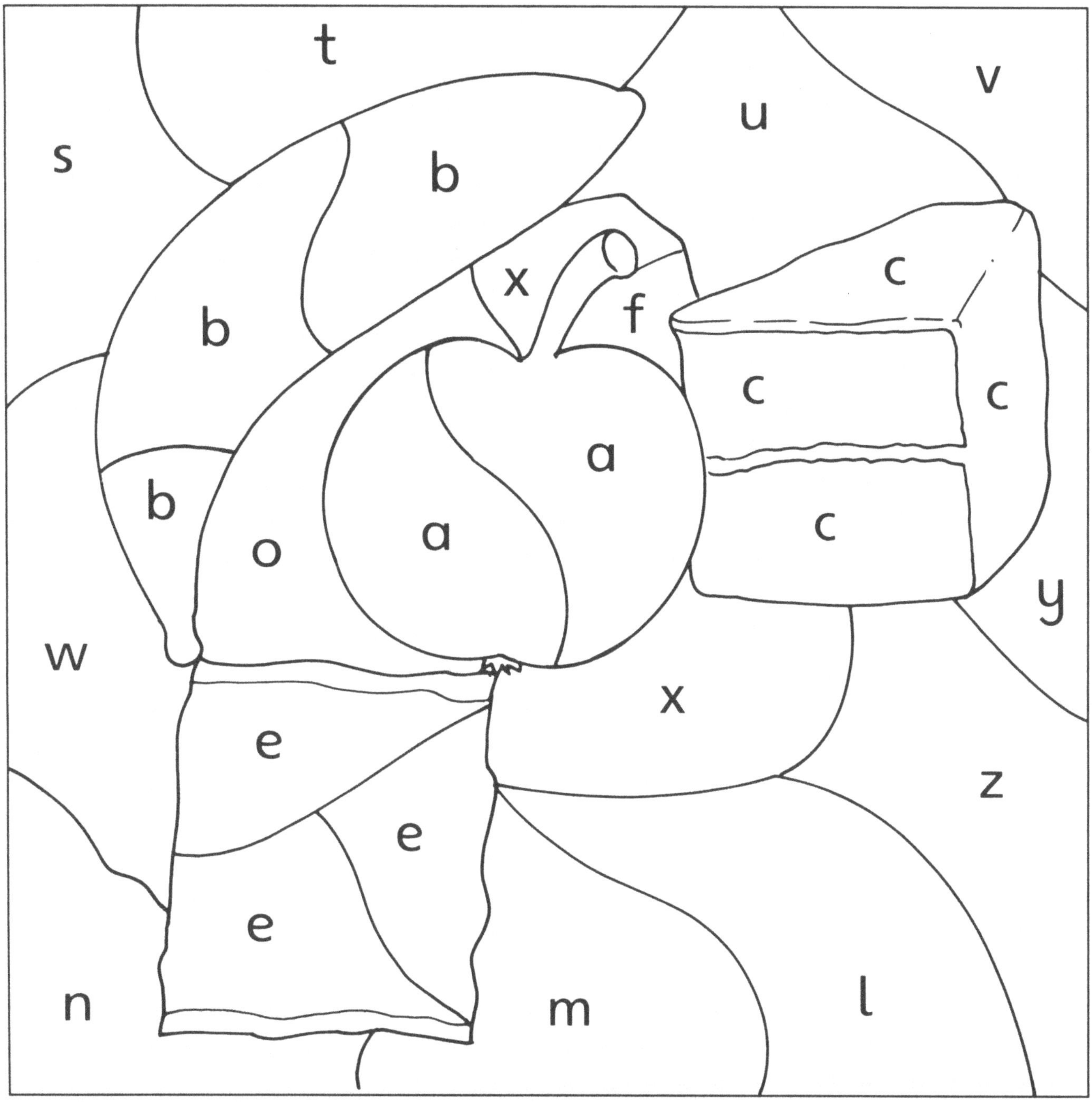

The empty lunch box

Skill: Letter and colour recognition

Instructions: Colour the big letters the correct colours. Then colour the shapes to match the letters.

Write over the correct word.

'My lunch is *not / can* here!'

Jess *you / went* up to Mrs Patel.

Tom went *up / in* to Mrs Patel.

Adam went up *here / to* Mrs Patel.

'Now *you / here* can eat,' said Jess.

'Yes I can,' *went / said* Mrs Patel.

The empty lunch box

Skill: Reading for meaning and sight word recognition
Instructions: Read the sentence. Write over the correct word. Then colour the pictures.

Make the rainbow letters.

The see-saw

Skill: Letter/sound discrimination and letter formation
Instructions: Use three different colours to make a 'rainbow' letter. Colour the pictures that start with the letter sound.

Who is speaking?

'I want to go on the see-saw,' said Tom. / Jess.

'You can't go on the see-saw,' said Tom. / Jess.

'We are on it,' said Tom. / Jess.

'I like it up here,' said Tom. / Adam.

'Can I go on the see-saw now?' said Jess. / Adam.

'No, you can't,' said Jess. / Tom.

'I can go on here,' said Adam. / Tom.

'Help!' said Jess. / Adam.

The see-saw

Skill: Word recognition and story recall

Instructions: Read the sentence. Look back through the story then circle the character who is speaking.

Find the rhyme.

like

eat

am

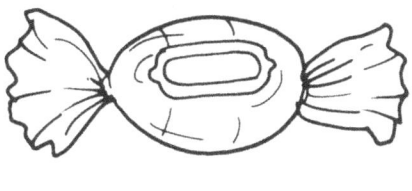 can

said

now

and

2

stop

you

but

The robots

Skill: Rhyme recognition and sight vocabulary
Instructions: Draw a line to join the sight word to its rhyming picture.

Make the words.

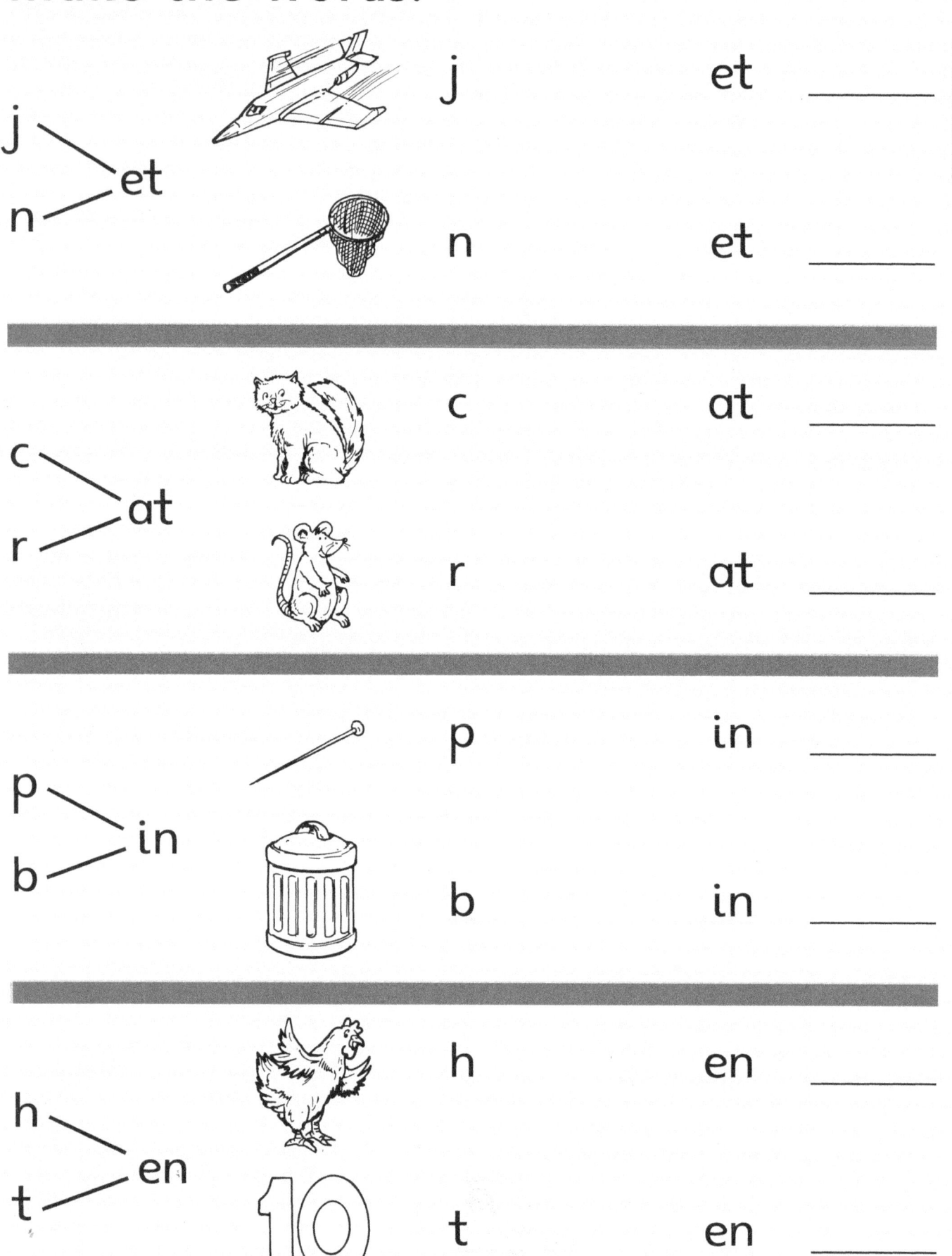

j
n >et

j et ___
n et ___

c
r >at

c at ___
r at ___

p
b >in

p in ___
b in ___

h
t >en

h en ___
t en ___

The robots

Skill: Onset and rime

Instructions: Complete the words, first write the endings and then write the beginnings. Then write the whole word.

Jess
stories
Stage 3

Name

Go over the letters.

a a a a a a a a

c c c c c c c c

d d d d d d d d

g g g g g g g g

o o o o o o o o

Heinemann

The lost coat

Skill: Letter formation

Finish the sentences.

'This is not my coat,' said Tom.

'This is not ___ coat,' ____ Tom.

'This _ __ __ coat,' ___ Tom.

'It is too big,' ___ Tom.

'It _ too __,' said Tom.

'It _ __ __,' said Tom.

The lost coat